CAPE TOW
FAIREST CAPE

• CAPE TOWN •

ON A CLEAR DAY...

Table Mountain, named for its flat top and steep sides, is spectacular in any weather, but when the southeaster drapes it in a tablecloth of cloud, it is not difficult to imagine a pantheon of cliff gods sitting down for a banquet. There are two methods of gaining access to its summit *(top)*: the sedentary way, via the five-minute cable-car ride *(left)* and the more strenuous way, on foot up one of the paths, the easiest and most used of which winds up Platteklip Gorge *(opposite left)*.

Rock dassies *(bottom left)*, shy elsewhere, have become accustomed to visitors to their mountain domain; although they appear harmless, they are capable of delivering a nasty – and decidedly unhygienic – nip.

• TABLE MOUNTAIN •

Table Mountain is clothed in unique fynbos finery, the best known specimen of which is undoubtedly the magnificent king protea *(opposite centre)*, South Africa's national flower.

From the top of the mountain, visitors are treated to a 360-degree spectacle of some of the most breathtaking views in the world, from Cape Point in the south to the blue peaks of the Hottentot Hollands range far in the east. Directly below is the generous sweep of Table Bay and the city itself, appearing toy-like from the mountain summit's 1 086-metre-high vantage point. Table Mountain, protective as she is of Cape Town, has a brooding side: the weather can close in suddenly and unexpectedly, and it is not unusual for walkers to become lost in the network of paths or climbers to fall from the cliffs.

• CAPE TOWN •

MARKETS AND MONUMENTS

The city, a hive of industry by day *(above left)* and a vista of lights by night *(opposite page, top left)*, is a fascinating amalgamation of high-powered business and informal-sector trading. Sandwiched between office blocks and turn-of-the-century buildings are flamboyant pockets of hawkers that sell everything from fresh produce to used CDs. The flower sellers on Adderley Street *(left)* lend colour, perfume and cheerful banter to the city's more formal daytime persona. Cobblestoned Greenmarket Square *(above right)*, once the trading place of market gardeners, is today packed to capacity with a kaleidoscope of vendors selling handmade and secondhand goods. Facing the square is the Old Town House, repository of the Michaelis Collection of old Dutch and Flemish oil paintings; it began life in 1755 as the Burgher Watch House, later became the headquarters of the town's police force and, from 1840 until 1905, served as the City Hall.

• CITY CENTRE •

Cape Town's founding father, Jan van Riebeeck, keeps guard over the city that grew from the small victualling station he established at the southern tip of Africa in 1652. His statue *(left)* stands on the Foreshore, created by the reclamation of land from the sea; the dredging operations for the development removed almost eight kilometres of sandy beach from Table Bay's western shoreline. A bridge across the centuries is the Civic Centre, an imposing building echoing the severe lines of the mountain – which are, unfortunately, rendered far better by nature than by man – and which is fronted by a stark, open plaza the focal point on which is a red-pipework modern-art statement called The Knot *(right)* created by contemporary sculptor Edoardo Villa.

• CAPE TOWN •

CITY CITADEL

The oldest occupied building in South Africa, the Castle of Good Hope dates back to the 1670s, when the Atlantic Ocean crashed against its bastions; today, it is separated from the sea by a raised motorway and a maze of railway lines, part of the Foreshore reclamation of the 1940s. Built by the Dutch in the shape of a pentagon, its five bastions – the better to protect the fledgling colony from attack from both land and sea – were named after the titles of the Prince of Orange. Through the centuries, criminals, military men and titled ladies have crossed its moat *(opposite page, top left)* to enter through the brickwork gateway commissioned by Governor Simon van der Stel in the late 1600s *(above right)* and walk the cobbled central square *(above)*.

• HISTORIC CAPE TOWN •

The most striking feature within the courtyard is the graceful Kat Balcony, which dates back to 1695 and is believed to be the work of the celebrated architect Louis Thibault and master craftsman Anton Anreith. Added to and altered through the following decades, and finally restored in the early 1990s, today the Castle serves primarily as a museum.

General Jan Smuts, South Africa's wartime prime minister and world statesman, whose statue *(opposite bottom left)* stands at the base of Wale Street outside the Cultural History Museum, was known to enjoy walking on Table Mountain. His favourite route on the mountain, which ascends Skeleton Gorge from Kirstenbosch Gardens to Maclear's Beacon, was named in his honour.

The Dutch Reformed Groote Kerk *(above right)* on Church Square first opened its doors in 1704, and remained a haven for worshipers for 130 years, until it was demolished. Of the original church, only the steeple remains; the new church, reopened in 1841, boasts a wooden pulpit carved by Anton Anreith.

• CAPE TOWN •

ON THE CITY'S FRINGE

The Company's Garden, originally a vegetable patch planted more than 300 years ago to replenish the stocks of visiting ships, today is a leafy retreat from the city, boasting more than 8 000 species of tree, shrub and flower, as well as tearooms and fishponds, tame squirrels and doves, statues and museums. A stroll down the oak-lined Government Avenue *(right)* will take you past the South African Library, the Houses of Parliament, Tuynhuis (the State President's town residence), the National Gallery, the twin-towered Great Synagogue *(above)* and the South African Museum *(above right)*.

• CITY BOWL •

Bo-Kaap *(left)*, on the lower slopes of Signal Hill, was once known as the 'Malay Quarter'. It is home to many of the city's large Muslim community, most of whom are descended from slaves and exiles sent to the Cape from Java over three centuries ago. The cries of the muezzins calling from the mosques' minarets are part and parcel of this historic slice of Cape Town. Its exotic setting of quaint, flat-roofed, 18th-century houses is enlivened further during the annual Minstrel Carnival *(above)*, when exuberant, banjo-playing singers and dancers gather in troupes and parade through the city on New Year's Day.

• CAPE TOWN •

• WATERFRONT •

TAVERN OF THE SEAS

The Victoria & Alfred Waterfront is one of Cape Town's most popular attractions. The massive development, on the site of the historic harbour, linked the city with the sea for the first time in 50 years. It combines modern function in a luxury marina, and its many shopping arcades, theatre and cinema complexes, hotels, restaurants and pubs, with old-fashioned form in the painstaking mimicry and restoration of turn-of-the-century architectural styles. The Clock Tower Precinct *(opposite)*, opened in 2001 by Nelson Mandela, includes the Robben Island Gateway, from which the ferries *Makana* and *Autshumato* leave hourly each day.

11

• CAPE TOWN •

SHIPS AND SHOPS

The recreational section of the Victoria & Alfred Waterfront offers a huge variety of inviting restaurants, cafés and pubs for those wishing to relax and have a meal. At Quay Four *(left)* visitors can watch seals playing and tourist vessels and private yachts come and go in Victoria Basin, while they enjoy alfresco delicacies.

In the historic Portswood Ridge area of the Waterfront, visitors can see the Time Ball Tower *(above)*. Navigators on ships in the harbour would watch the time ball and set their clocks as it dropped.

• WATERFRONT •

PIER PLEASURE

At the Victoria Wharf *(above)* retailers in established shops do business in tandem with informal traders who sell their wares from barrows and carts reminiscent, as is the building itself, of a bygone, Victorian era. The Wharf looks out onto the Victoria (outer) Basin, built between 1893 and 1895. Today it is berth to a range of pleasurecraft, including ferries that offer visitors short, inshore tours. The plaza outside the Victoria Wharf is a favourite spot for buskers, street theatre and mime artists *(right)*, although any open space in the Waterfront provides an ad-hoc platform for these impromptu entertainers. Minstrels get feet tapping on the Pierhead *(above right)*, one of the first areas in the Waterfront to be restored and upgraded – fittingly, as the first public building to be constructed on the old Pierhead, in 1903, was the beloved Harbour Café. The old Port Captain's Building, seen behind the minstrels, dates back to 1904.

• CAPE TOWN •

SURF CITY

The suburbs on the Atlantic seaboard, to the north of Cape Town, represent the city's older seaside face. Seapoint *(above right)*, once a magnet to weekend revellers with its 'golden mile' of restaurants *(above)* and nightclubs, today is more subdued, much of its patronage having been drawn to the new Victoria & Alfred Waterfront development. Highrise buildings and shops, and Victorian homes and more modern, small apartment blocks, stand side by side in this suburb on the slopes of Signal Hill. Although the Atlantic Ocean is on the 'cold' side of the Peninsula, divers and surfers flock to its waters, donning wetsuits before plunging into the icy surf *(right)* off Clifton Beach at the foot of Lion's Head. In summer, Clifton's beautiful beaches attract sunworshippers in droves. They are also a favourite with the after-work brigade, who enjoy sundowners in the late-evening twilight.

14

• ATLANTIC SEABOARD •

SUMMER FUN

Heading away from Seapoint, Clifton and the city, the winding road hugs a narrow strip of coast in the shadow of the Twelve Apostles, an extension of the Table Mountain range. Here some of the most sought-after real estate in the country can be found in suburbs like up-market Camps Bay *(above right)*, with its lawned beachside walk, tidal pools and palm trees, and the picturesque, cliffside village of Llandudno *(right)*. The white-sand sweeps of beach along this stretch attract hordes of visitors during the summer months, although none but the hardiest (or hottest) brave the icy waters.

• CAPE TOWN •

WHERE LEOPARDS ONCE ROAMED

H out Bay, with its village atmosphere and bustling little harbour, is considered – particularly by its residents – a place apart. Once a thickly forested valley hemmed in between the mountains and the sea, the bronze leopard *(left)* that overlooks the harbour is a reminder that big cats once roamed the forests and hills of the area. Hout Bay has always housed a community of fishermen, as far back as the Stone Age, when Strandlopers lived in caves above the then high-water mark. Today the tradition continues: the Mariner's Wharf is a favourite venue for seafood lovers, who throng to its restaurants and fish shops for freshly caught delights.

• HOUT BAY •

BIRD'S-EYE VIEW

For those with the time and effort to spare, the numerous walks and trails in the hills and mountains around Hout Bay provide stunning views over the bay and the little village *(above)*. The kilometre-long sweep of beach gives onto water that is often warmer than that of the more exposed beaches, and is popular with parents with small children. For the more sedentary, there are a number of pleasant restaurants in the village, not least of which is the historic Kronendal *(above right)*, on the Main Road and much at home in its beautiful Cape Dutch gabled building.

• CAPE TOWN •

MOUNTAIN AND SEA

The famous Chapman's Peak Drive *(above)*, closed at times due to the danger of rockfalls, is about ten kilometres of twisting and turning road clinging to the cliffside along the Peninsula's western edge between Hout Bay and the northern end of Noordhoek Beach. An unforgettable sight from this road is that of the magnificent sweep of Long Beach *(opposite page)*, an eight-kilometre stretch frequented by horseriders, ramblers and surfers – although when the summer southeaster howls along its length, it is likely to be deserted. Its waters are cold and treacherous, and are more likely to be favoured by fishermen than by swimmers. The baboons that inhabit this part of the Peninsula are overfriendly and can be threatening – don't feed or tease them.

CHAPMAN'S PEAK TO NOORDHOEK

• CAPE TOWN •

TAKING THE POINT

The Cape of Good Hope Nature Reserve, a 7 750-hectare sanctuary for indigenous flora and fauna, was originally proclaimed in 1939 for the preservation of the Cape mountain zebra and the bontebok *(right)*, both endangered species. The waters off the reserve, while not great for swimming or surfing, are a diver's paradise *(above right)*. From the elevated vantage of Cape Point *(above)*, visitors can spot seals and dolphins gambolling in the waves and sometimes, if they're lucky, a submerged whale.

• CAPE POINT •

The southernmost tip of the Peninsula is, however, actually the Cape of Good Hope *(above right)*, and not Cape Point as is commonly believed. The sandy bay between these two capes is named in memory of Bartolomeu Dias, who holds the honour of being the first navigator to round the Cape of Good Hope, in 1488, en route to Algoa Bay. On his return journey he planted one of his granite *padrões*, or crosses, a replica of which stands near Buffelsbaai. The Vasco da Gama cross *(right)*, erected above Bordjiesrif, is not only a monument to this great Portuguese seaman, but also a beacon warning ships off the rocky coastline.

Smitswinkelbaai *(above)* is an isolated little haven of seaside cottages, access to which is gained by a very steep and treacherous-looking path off the road to Cape Point. Although the cove with its pocket-handkerchief beach offers safe swimming, it is right in the path of the blustering summer southeaster.

• CAPE TOWN •

NAVAL TRADITIONS

Simon's Town, the second harbour and settlement at the Cape, was originally used by the British as a bridgehead for their occupation of the colony in 1795; in 1814 it was proclaimed the South Atlantic Station for Britain's Royal Navy; and in 1957 it was handed over to the South African Navy. Residences, running the gamut of architectural styles from charming 18th-century neo-classical structures to more modern dwellings, line the main street of this little village and echo its long connection with the ocean.

• SIMON'S TOWN •

PENGUINS ON PARADE

Boulders *(above)*, a succession of sandy coves just south of the town, offers warm, shallow water for children and deep, calm water for stronger swimmers. An added attraction is the colony of Jackass Penguins that lives in the area – it is not unusual to have one amble over your towel while you're sunbathing. Naval nostalgia is the order of the day at the Simon's Town Museum *(above right)*, housed in The Residency, which dates back to 1977. A monument to Able Seaman Just Nuisance *(right)*, a Great Dane that befriended British sailors during the Second World War, holds pride of place in Jubilee Square.

• CAPE TOWN •

False Bay

DAYTRIPPERS' DELIGHT

The warm waters that lap the False Bay coast attract beach enthusiasts of all ages. The little fishing centre of Kalk Bay *(right)* takes its name from the lime ('kalk') kilns that were built in the area in the late 1700s, to burn shells for the production of whitewash. In 1806 the harbour became the centre of a British whaling operation. Today some of its main attractions are the bustling fishing harbour, the antique and craft shops, and the sea-edge pub and restaurant, the Brass Bell – those who overindulge on the wine can meander outside to the neighbouring railway station and catch a scenic train ride home.

St James *(above left)*, one of the few havens on the Peninsula not battered by the summer southeaster, is well known for its beach, tidal pool and brightly coloured changing booths *(opposite page, right)*.

24

• FALSE BAY •

It is difficult to imagine, when the summertime fun lovers flock to the shores of Muizenberg and turn the beach into a festival of colour and movement, that this was the scene of the 1795 battle between the British and the Dutch which culminated in the first British occupation of the Cape.

In 1883, when the suburban railway linked the village to Cape Town, it became one of the most desirable seaside resorts in the British Empire. Today the spacious beachfront at Muizenberg and its candy-striped pavilion *(above)* continue to attract day trippers from far and wide.

• CAPE TOWN •

FRUITS OF THE VINE

The wine regions that spread across the southwestern Cape like a patchwork quilt grew from the little vineyards established on the slopes of Table Mountain, in the Company's Garden, by the hardy burghers of the 1600s. The French Huguenots carried the art of wine-making both further afield and to new heights. Today, three wine farms form the Cape Peninsula wine route: Groot Constantia, Klein Constantia and Buitenverwachting. It was on the historic estate Groot Constantia *(above left)* that Governor Simon van der Stel produced the first successful wines to come out of the Cape. The estate, which continues to produce fine red and white wines, is today a national monument and boasts the gracious Cape Dutch homestead, restored to its former glory

26

• CONSTANTIA WINE ROUTE •

and furnished in 18th-century style *(opposite, bottom right)*, a wine museum housed in the old wine cellar *(above)*, which is graced with an original frieze designed by master craftsman Anton Anreith, and two popular restaurants, the more casual of which is the Jonkershuis *(opposite, bottom left)*. Tours through the modern, double-storeyed cellar take place daily, on the hour. The smaller, more private estate of Klein Constantia *(far right)* also boasts vineyards that survive from Van der Stel's time.

27

• CAPE TOWN •

CAPE FLORAL KINGDOM

The southwestern tip of the Western Cape, cut off as it is from the rest of Africa by its barrier of mountains, is in more ways than one a world apart. In this very limited area is found the smallest and yet the richest of the world's seven floral kingdoms. Many of the shrubs feature small, tightly rolled leaves, which led to the Dutch appellation '*fijnbosch*' and, ultimately, to its modern name, fynbos. Protea species abound in many shapes and forms,

KIRSTENBOSCH

from the colourful, red-tipped pincushions to the glittery-leaved silver tree *(opposite, top left)*; the genus was named after the Greek sea god Proteus, who could change his shape at will. Ground orchids in all colours of the rainbow abound on Table Mountain, the most prized of which is the red disa *(opposite, right)*, the emblem of the Western Cape. To see the Cape flora at its flowering best, a trip to the Kirstenbosch National Botanic Gardens *(opposite, bottom right; above and right)* in spring is called for. Visitors can give their senses a treat by following the braille trail that runs through the fragrance garden, and spend many delightful hours wandering the well-paved paths between the rolling lawns and meticulously laid-out gardens.

• CAPE TOWN •

RHODES' LEGACY

One of the Cape's most illustrious citizens was empire-builder and statesman Cecil John Rhodes *(left)*. On his death, he bequeathed part of his large estate, Groote Schuur, to the University of Cape Town. The oldest university in Africa, it had its formative years on the other side of the mountain, in Orange Street near the Company's Garden, and moved to this beautifully scenic site below Devil's Peak *(above)* in 1928. The university overlooks Mostert's Mill *(right)*, a pretty reminder of the Cape's Dutch links. It was built in 1796 to grind wheat and was restored in 1936.

• GROOTE SCHUUR ESTATE •

Rhodes' Memorial *(above right)*, in the centre of the original Groote Schuur Estate, with its bronze lions and equestrian statue 'Energy', is a striking granite example of imperial architecture, and affords panoramic views over the Cape Flats. A walk through Newlands Forest *(above left)*, abutting the university campus, is a treat for tree lovers, with specimens of cherrywood, wild olive and mountain saffron, among others, shading the way.

A memorable way to get the full measure of the Peninsula *(overleaf)* is from a helicopter, many of which operate on a charter basis out of the Victoria & Alfred Waterfront. From the air, the sandstone massif of Table Mountain, with Devil's Peak to the west and Lion's Head and Signal Hill to the east, forms the central focus of the spiny mountain chain that runs to Cape Point. Here, the City of Cape Town is revealed in all its splendour.

CAPE TOWN